Cuttings
Made Clear

A COMPLETE GUIDE TO TAKING CUTTINGS

by Beatrice C. Hearne

FISONS
Clearcut
INSTRUCTIONS

CLEARCUT* is an easy-to-use gel in pots specially made for rooting cuttings. The gel pots are ready to use – simply take your cutting, insert into the gel, and pot up when well rooted.

*Correct method and plant material are important for success.
* Suitable for softwood (green stem) cuttings, but **not** for hardwood (brown stem) cuttings.
* CLEARCUT does not make cuttings root faster, some will root within a week whilst others may need up to six weeks.
* To help you succeed with CLEARCUT details on taking cuttings are given below.

1 TAKING CUTTINGS

Choose healthy plants, and take cuttings from parts of the plants which are actively growing and without flowers.

Use a clean sharp knife when preparing cuttings. Many soft-wood (green stem) cuttings will root in CLEARCUT. Therefore most houseplants, half-hardy perennials (such as Fuchsia or Perlargoniums), border perennials, and softwood cuttings from some shrubs will root in the gel. CLEARCUT is not recommended for hardwood cuttings.

Insert cuttings into the gel immediately after preparation to avoid wilting. Up to four cuttings may be put into each pot depending on the size of the cutting.

There are many different types of cuttings to suit a variety of plants. Take cuttings in the normal way and at the correct time of year – refer to gardening books if you are in doubt. However here is a brief guide on how to take a few of the many types of cuttings which can be used with CLEARCUT.

Leaf cuttings

For some plants with larger leaves and little or no stem such as Sansevieria, Begonia Rex, Cape Primrose, Gloxinia etc. Select a healthy adult leaf and cut sections 1" or more in height across the leaf, including a main vein, and trim if necessary. Insert the cutting upright about halfway into the gel. For succulents such as Sedum and Sempervivum etc., detach a whole leaf, trim and insert about halfway into the gel. Roots and a new plant will form from the base of the _____

Stem cuttings

For a wide variety of plants including Geranium, Fuchsia, Chrysanthemum, Philodendron, Coleus, Tradescantia, Grape Ivy, Poinsettia and softwood cuttings from shrubs, etc. Choose a healthy young shoot, 2 to 4 inches long. Trim leaves from the lower half of the stem (including any unhealthy leaves), trim to just below a leaf joint and insert about halfway into the gel.

Leaf stem cuttings

For leaves of African Violet, Peperomia and some small-leaved Begonias, etc. Use a healthy adult leaf with its stem, trim and insert up to the leaf in the gel. Roots will grow from the stem and a new plant will grow from the base of the leaf.

Bud cuttings

For plants with short stem sections and a bud at each leaf joint or node such as Ivies, Ficus, etc. Remove a section of stem by cutting above and below a leaf joint. Insert the stem section below the bud into the gel. Roots will form from the stem in the gel and a new plant will _____ d at the leaf joint.

encourage disease. Ensure that there is good contact between the cutting and the gel and that the cutting is supported by the gel. A rooting hormone can be used in the normal way before insertion if desired. This will improve success rate.

KEEP THE POTS WITH CUTTINGS IN A LIGHT, WARM, BUT WELL VENTILATED PLACE, AVOIDING DIRECT SUNLIGHT.

After a few days the gel may begin to dry out slightly, however this is normal and will not affect rooting so long as the cutting has been inserted properly.

It is not recommended to re-use the gel pots. However if the cuttings root quickly and are easily removed then the product can be re-used. If for any reason the gel has become uneven in transport or contains large air bubbles, gently tap the pot on a firm surface to restore an even surface on the gel.

CLEARCUT is completely safe to use – even for children.

3 POTTING UP

When you can see that cuttings are well rooted, cut away the foil and carefully remove cuttings from the pot. Do not remove the gel residue around the roots as the cuttings will benefit from this protective layer of gel which will help them grow. Plant them in Fisons Levington* compost in the normal way. Levington composts are peat based with a _____

A Fisons Publication

Production: Inmerc BV, Wormer (Holland) and Mercurius (U.K.) Ltd.,
Colchester, Essex
Horticultural advisors: R. W. Daniels, T. Challenger, C. Griffiths,
J. Pertwee
Photography: APS, Ardleigh, Essex; Fleurmerc BV, Wormerveer
(Holland); J.B. Presentations Ltd., *Practical Gardening* and the Ann Tree
Collection
Drawings: Ben Schoonhein, Maarssen (Holland); APS, Ardleigh, Essex
Lay-out: Loek de Leeuw (Inmerc BV); Willemijn Brandes, Muiderberg
(Holland)
Cover design: APS, Ardleigh, Essex
Type-setting: Fotoset BV, Wormerveer (Holland)
Lithography: Basisscan BV, Amsterdam (Holland)
Printing: BV Kunstdrukkerij Mercurius-Wormeerveer (Holland)
© Fisons plc, 1986

Contents

Introduction

Taking cuttings is one of the easiest and most popular ways to grow new plants of many kinds. For many plant species, taking cuttings is the only way to propagate a new plant exactly like the parent plant. Millions of people take cuttings every year from both indoor and outdoor plants, surprisingly more people than buy seeds. Cuttings can also be a fast way to grow new plants. Often a cutting can be rooted and potted up within 4-6 weeks, and grown into an adult plant in less than six months.

Cuttings also save money. They offer an inexpensive way to grow several new plants from one, for your own house or garden, or to give or exchange with family, friends and neighbours. Most of all, taking cuttings can be a hobby for anyone. You need only to have one houseplant to start, or you may have a large garden to fill with new plants. There are several different types of cuttings to suit a wide variety of plants. The two main types are softwood and hardwood cuttings, and within these there are specific ways to prepare

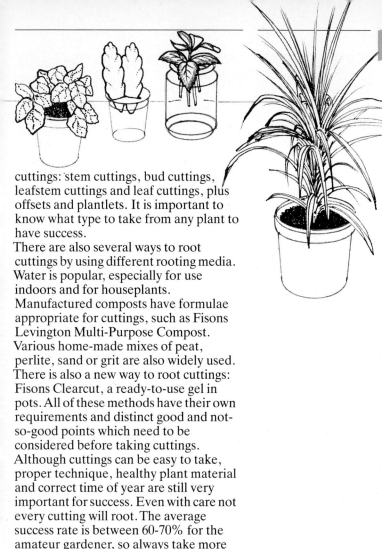

cuttings: stem cuttings, bud cuttings, leafstem cuttings and leaf cuttings, plus offsets and plantlets. It is important to know what type to take from any plant to have success.

There are also several ways to root cuttings by using different rooting media. Water is popular, especially for use indoors and for houseplants. Manufactured composts have formulae appropriate for cuttings, such as Fisons Levington Multi-Purpose Compost. Various home-made mixes of peat, perlite, sand or grit are also widely used. There is also a new way to root cuttings: Fisons Clearcut, a ready-to-use gel in pots. All of these methods have their own requirements and distinct good and not-so-good points which need to be considered before taking cuttings. Although cuttings can be easy to take, proper technique, healthy plant material and correct time of year are still very important for success. Even with care not every cutting will root. The average success rate is between 60-70% for the amateur gardener, so always take more cuttings than you need.

This guide is designed to help explain all of the important things you need to know about cuttings. It also gives detailed information on how to take cuttings from over 190 plants. I hope the guide will make very clear indeed how to take cuttings successfully.

Beatrice C. Hearne
November 1986

How to take cuttings

Equipment
The basic equipment needed for taking cuttings by the average gardener or houseplant owner simply includes a sharp knife or secateurs, a rooting medium and a kitchen windowsill. The knife or secateurs should be clean in order to avoid disease, and sharp in order to make clean cuts without tearing or bruising either the cutting or the parent plant. The rooting medium should be purchased or made especially for cuttings, never recycled from other plant pots, or garden soil used in pots. A rooting hormone plus fungicide is also useful to encourage root formation and to help prevent fungus diseases.

Temperature control
A temperature of 18-21°C (65-70°F) is ideal for most cuttings although many will still do well between 15-21°C (55-70°F). Try to ensure that the temperature does not drop below 10°C (50°F), especially at night or during cold spells whether in the greenhouse, conservatory or on the

windowsill. Avoid drawing curtains between cuttings on the windowsill and the heating during colder months of the year as this 'cold shoulder' treatment will thoroughly discourage any plant and especially cuttings from rooting. More sophisticated equipment for propagation via cuttings can help increase success and reduce work needed for cuttings taken on a large scale. Propagators or greenhouses which provide temperature and moisture control are invaluable for providing conditions for cuttings to root during much of the year. 'Bottom' heat or gentle warmth supplied by electrical cables or tanks filled for example with hot water or oil to the base of pots or trays is a good way of encouraging rooting. Use any of the commonly available methods, which suit your own situation.

Remove flowers and flower buds from cuttings to conserve their energy for rooting.

Moisture control

During the summer months temperature control is usually less of a problem but then moisture or humidity control is important. Especially in the case of rooting in compost, cuttings are very sensitive to moisture loss. This is why direct sunlight is so damaging. One way to prevent serious dehydration is to enclose the cuttings in a clear polythene bag which is supported by canes or a wire frame above the pot or tray without touching the cuttings. This will help retain moisture while cuttings root. This treatment is not needed when using water or Clearcut to root softwood cuttings, or for hardwood cuttings with any rooting medium. Alternatively cuttings can be misted regularly with water via a hand-held sprayer to increase humidity on the leaves, just as established plants appreciate.

Other useful items
Labels – for date and identification of cuttings.
Dibber – for making holes in rooting media, to firm in cuttings, and to aid removal of cuttings when rooted in compost.
Rubber bands – for holding together leaves of large cuttings such as Ficus (Rubber plant) in order to save space and reduce moisture loss.

Methods

There are many different methods of
rooting cuttings by using different rooting
media.

A common method for house-
plants is water, usually in a jam jar or
similar small container. For outdoor
plants and half-hardy perennials such as
geraniums and fuchsias a widely
used method of rooting cuttings is
compost or mixtures of peat, sand, grit,
or vermiculite in varying quantities
according to need. However, these two
methods, water and compost, are often
interchangeable for many indoor and
outdoor plants. It is remarkable that

these rooting media are quite different in
all respects and yet are both able to
entice cuttings to root.

There are also several other methods of
rooting cuttings. A new method is Fisons
Clearcut, a clear gel in pots which is ready
to use. Some cuttings root in types of
polyurethane foam. In air-layering, moist
moss serves as a form of rooting medium,
and of course good garden soil is often
used in layering outdoors.

An easy way to propagate a low-growing shrub like Euonymus is to layer it. Firmly peg down lower stems into peaty soil in late summer. Separate new plants in spring.

The important thing to do is to choose the medium best suited to your plant or cuttings type and to the amount of maintenance you are willing to give.

Don't be afraid to experiment. Experimenting will help you discover the best method for your plants, your growing conditions and the time and effort you want to spend.

Here is a brief guide on how to use the popular types of rooting media plus some of their advantages and disadvantages.

Water

How to use it:
- take cuttings in the normal way, mainly from houseplants and half-hardy perennials;
- insert stem, leafstem or leaf at least halfway into the water;
- top up or replace the water when the level drops or when the water becomes cloudy or green.

Advantages:
- readily available;
- easy to use;
- good success rate for houseplants.

Disadvantages:
- suitable mainly for indoor plants (softwood cuttings);
- can cause rotting of 'hairy-stemmed' cuttings;
- needs regular topping up;
- encourages growth of algae and scum;
- slow establishment after potting up due to incorrect root structure.

Compost
How to use it:
- take cuttings in the normal way from all plant types;
- dust base with rooting hormone;
- insert cutting at least halfway into the compost and firm lightly;
- keep the compost moist and protect the cuttings from moisture loss;
- pot up when well rooted.

Advantages:
- readily available;
- nutrients are available once the cuttings begin to root.

Disadvantages:
- rooting progress cannot be seen;
- the compost dries out quickly, which can be damaging.

Clearcut gel
How to use it:
- take cuttings in the normal way, softwood only;
- dust base with rooting hormone;
- pierce foil and insert the cuttings at least halfway into the gel;
- pot up when well rooted.

Advantages:
- easy to use;
- no maintenance;
- gel on the roots helps in transplanting;
- the roots are visible.

Disadvantages:
- more costly than compost or water;
- suitable for softwood cuttings only.

Always select cuttings from a characteristic part of the parent plant.

Types of cuttings

There are many different ways to take cuttings. Cuttings are divided into groups depending on the kind of plant and the time of year best suited for them. It is very important to distinguish between the groups for success. The two main groups are **softwood** and **hardwood** cuttings. Each has its own requirements for rooting, although general rules always apply, such as correct size, sufficient warmth and moisture and the appropriate rooting medium.

Always select cuttings from a characteristic part of the parent plant so that your new plant reflects the desired colour and vigour of the parent. Care and attention to detail in taking cuttings correctly will be rewarded with strong healthy new plants.

Softwood cuttings

This is the type of cutting for many plants including houseplants, perennials and some shrubs, and they are usually taken in spring and summer. The cuttings are usually green in colour, although there are exceptions such as fuchsias which

Softwood cuttings should be soft young growth usually with green or pink stems. In each of these four examples the preferred cutting is on the right.

have a pink stem suitable for a softwood cutting. For best results take softwood cuttings between March and October for houseplants and perennials, and in June and July for shrubs. These cuttings root quickly, usually in anything from one to eight weeks. Softwood cuttings of tender or half-hardy plants, i.e. plants that are susceptible to frost, tend to be rooted indoors or in heated greenhouses. Use a rooting hormone with fungicide to encourage rooting.

How to select softwood cuttings:
- Young, immature sections, usually from the current season's growth.
- Firm but flexible shoots, not brittle or woody.
- Softwood stem cuttings should be at least two to four inches long including at least two leaf joints.
- Without flowers, fruit or seedheads.
- Always remove damaged, diseased or excess leaves.

If only woody stems or no stems without flowers or fruit are available, pinch out tips to encourage the plant to 'break' or form new shoots. Use these shoots for cuttings.

How to prepare softwood cuttings:
There are different types of softwood cuttings:

Stem cuttings. This is the most common type of cutting. Stem cuttings can be made from shoot tips or side shoots, and are taken from many plants with distinct

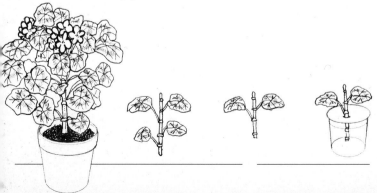

stems such as Pelargoniums (geraniums) and fuchsias, also from most shrubs. Choose a healthy young shoot, two to four inches long. Trim leaves from the lower half of the stem (including any unhealthy leaves), cut the stem to just below a leaf joint and insert at least half of the cutting into the rooting medium.

Leaf stem cuttings. Cuttings from plants consisting mainly of leaves with short stems or no distinct stems such as Saintpaulias (African violets) and some Peperomias.

Use a healthy adult leaf with its stem, trim and insert up to the leaf in the rooting medium. Roots will grow from the stem and a new plant will grow from the base of the leaf.

Bud cuttings. Suitable for plants with long trailing stems such as Hedera (Ivy) and Scindapsis (Grape ivy). Remove a section of the stem by cutting above and below a leaf joint. Insert the stem section below the bud into the rooting medium. Roots will be formed from the stem or a node and a new plant will grow from the bud at the leaf joint. This type of cutting can also be called a leaf eye cutting.

Leaf cuttings. For plants consisting mainly of leaves with little or no leaf stems such as Echeveria, or plants with very large leaves such as Sinningia (Gloxinia) or Sanseveria (Mother-in-law's tongue). Select an healthy adult leaf and cut sections of one inch or more in height across the leaf, including a main vein, and trim if necessary. Insert the cutting upright about halfway into the rooting medium. For succulents such as sedum and echeveria detach a whole leaf, trim and insert about halfway into the rooting medium. Roots and a new plant will be formed from the base of the leaf.

Offsets and plantlets. For plants which produce small immature sections which can be detached and grown on into an identical plant. Examples are Chlorophytum (Spider plant), Saxifraga and many cacti. Simply detach the offsets or plantlets and insert them in the rooting medium enough to support them.

Hardwood cuttings

This is the common type of cutting for many shrubs, trees and conifers, and they are usually taken in autumn and winter when growth is slowing down or dormant. Their stems are usually brown in colour. Take semi-hardwood cuttings between July and October and hardwood cuttings between September and March. These cuttings root slowly, in anything from two to twelve months. Hardwood cuttings are primarily for hardy plants, and tend to be rooted in containers out-of-doors in cold greenhouses, frames, or direct into prepared soil. Use a rooting hormone to encourage rooting.

How to select semi-hardwood cuttings:
- Take shoots of maturing growth from the current season's growth, usually basal (lower) parts of stems or shoots.
- Take firm shoots, woody at the base.
- Semi-hardwood stem cuttings should be three to ten inches long (depending on the parent plant size) including at least two leaf joints.
- Take shoots without flowers, fruit or seedheads.
- Always remove dead, damaged or excess leaves.

How to select hardwood cuttings:
- Take shoots of mature growth, usually basal parts of stems.

- Take firm and woody shoots (whole cutting).
- Hardwood stem cuttings should be six to eighteen inches long (depending on the parent plant size) including at least two leaf joints.
- Take shoots without flowers, fruit or seedheads.
- Buds in leaf axils should be firm and showing colour, usually pink or green.
- Always remove dead, damaged or excess leaves.

How to prepare hardwood cuttings:
There are three types of semi-hardwood and hardwood cuttings:

Stem cuttings. For most semi-hardwood and hardwood cuttings for conifers, shrubs and trees. Choose a firm woody stem at least six inches long, depending on the plant size.
Remove leaves from the lower part of the cutting. Trim to just below a leaf joint. Insert at least two-thirds of the cutting into the rooting medium. Alternatively take semi-hardwood cuttings with a 'heel' or a piece of mature wood off the main stem.

Bud or leaf bud cuttings. Suitable for most climbers and some evergreen shrubs and trees. Remove a section of the stem three to six inches long by cutting above and below a leaf joint.

Insert the stem up to the bud into the rooting medium. Roots will be formed from the stem and a new plant will grow from the bud at the leaf joint.

These cuttings are sometimes known as petiole cuttings, particularly for some evergreen shrubs such as Camellias and Rhododendrons. Only a very small section of the stem is required to include the bud and leaf. Carefully slice a 'shield' shaped section of the stem from the main stem to include the leaf and bud and insert this into the rooting medium.

<u>Root cuttings</u>. For some herbaceous perennials, shrubs and trees with fleshy roots such as Papaver (Poppy) and Syringa (Lilac). Lift the herbaceous plant or remove soil around a larger plant to expose the roots. Remove sections of root which are at least a quarter of an inch in diameter or approximately the same thickness as a pencil. Cut the roots into sections of one and a half to three inches long, using a flat or horizontal cut at the top end of the cutting and a sloping or diagonal cut at the bottom of the cutting. This serves as a guide to ensure the cuttings are inserted the right way up in the rooting medium. Insert the cuttings completely into the rooting medium. Shoots will be formed from the top of the cutting and roots from the sides and base. This type of cutting is taken in the dormant period and only suitable for a limited number of plants.

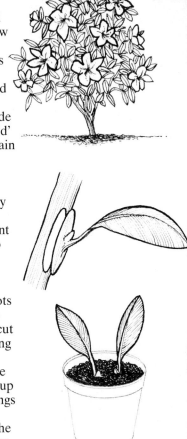

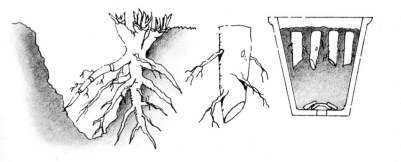

Cuttings calendar

The time of the year you choose to take cuttings is very important for success. This is a general guide on the best months for taking cuttings from different types of plants. Exact timing will depend on the specific plant, geographical location, and facilities available. At any time of the year make sure that the parent plant is healthy and for softwood cuttings is actively growing. For outdoor plants this usually means after late April/early May. But for houseplants it is more difficult. If you are unsure, bring it into a warmer place and give it a good watering and plant food at least a fortnight before taking cuttings. All cuttings appreciate protection from frost under glass and all softwood cuttings need a minimum temperature of 10°C (50°F). For details on specific plants, consult the cuttings guide.

January:
- root cuttings of some herbaceous perennials, shrubs and trees, protected under glass.

February:
- root cuttings of some herbaceous perennials, shrubs and trees, protected under glass;
- softwood stem cuttings from overwintered half-hardy perennials, including Pelargoniums (Geraniums) and hardy perennials such as carnations and Chrysanthemums.

March:
- softwood stem cuttings from overwintered half-hardy perennials, including Pelargoniums (Geraniums), Dahlias and Fuchsias;
- basal stem cuttings from border perennials;
- cuttings from houseplants;
- hardwood cuttings from shrubs.

April
- basal stem cuttings from border

Begonia, a leaf stem cutting.

perennials and half-hardy perennials such as Chrysanthemums and Dahlias;
- houseplants;
- softwood cuttings from shrubs.

May
- basal stem cuttings from border perennials such as Lupins and Delphiniums;
- alpines;
- houseplants, cacti and succulents;
- softwood cuttings from shrubs and climbers;
- herbs.

June:
- alpines;
- houseplants, cacti and succulents;
- softwood cuttings from shrubs and climbers;
- herbs.

July:
- stem cuttings from herbaceous (border) perennials and semi-

hardwood cuttings from shrubs and
trees;
- softwood cuttings from shrubs and
climbers;
- alpines;
- houseplants, cacti and succulents;
- herbs.

August:
- stem cuttings from herbaceous
(border) perennials and half-hardy
perennials including Pelargoniums
(Geraniums) and Fuchsias;
- softwood and semi-hardwood cuttings
from shrubs and climbers;
- alpines;
- houseplants, cacti and succulents;
- herbs;
- Strawberry runners.

September:
- stem cuttings from herbaceous
(border) perennials and half-hardy
perennials for overwintering, including
Pelargoniums (Geraniums) and
Fuchsias;
- alpines;
- houseplants, cacti and succulents;
- herbs;
- semi-hardwood cuttings from shrubs,
trees and climbers.

October:
- houseplants;
- semi-hardwood and hardwood cuttings
from shrubs, trees and climbers.

November:
- root cuttings of some herbaceous
(border) perennials, shrubs and trees,
protected under glass;
- hardwood cuttings from shrubs, trees
and climbers.

December:
- root cuttings of some herbaceous
(border) perennials, shrubs and trees
protected under glass;
- stem cuttings from perennial
Carnations and Chrysanthemums
protected under glass.

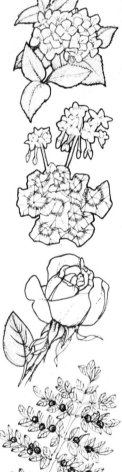

Success with cuttings

Success with cuttings is one of nature's lotteries. While professional plant growers can sometimes expect 100% success with many plants, they also provide the perfect environment, exact timing and often high technology to achieve their results. Even without these aids the amateur gardener can also achieve very high success rates if a few basic rules and techniques are followed. However one guarantee of getting the new plants you want is to take more cuttings than you need. Sometimes, even after the best care, cuttings fail to root. You should be able to find out the cause or many of the causes and avoid them next time. This chapter is intended to help identify some of the many reasons for failure and to suggest how to avoid them. In addition to a general checklist there is information on pests and diseases, some special tips and ideas, and details on potting up and cultivation, the important final stage of growing healthy new plants from cuttings.

Sansevieria, a leaf cutting.

Checklist

If your cuttings die or fail to root, these are some of the general points to consider before taking further cuttings:

– *Use plants suitable for propagation from cuttings.*

You must use plants that can be grown from cuttings and the best type of cutting for the plant. While the majority of houseplants and many garden plants and shrubs do grow from cuttings, there are also many plants which do not have the capability to form roots from stems or leaves. You simply must know or find out which plants are best for taking cuttings. Refer to the cuttings guide for details on 190 plants that are relatively easy to grow from cuttings.

– *Take cuttings at the correct time of year.*

In general this is March to October (spring and summer) for softwood cuttings, and October to March (autumn and winter) for semi-hardwood and hardwood cuttings. Again refer to the cuttings guide for details.

For softwood cuttings in particular the best rule is that the parent plant should be actively growing. Therefore avoid taking these cuttings between October and March, as during the winter months low temperatures encourage dormancy and disease and reduce rooting ability. For hardwood cuttings plants need not be in active growth as these are taken in autumn and winter.

– *Make sure that the cuttings are in good condition.*

Always start with healthy plants. Take cuttings neatly and cleanly, avoiding damage such as tearing or bruising, either when taking from the parent plant, preparing or when inserting the cutting into the rooting medium. In compost use a dibber to make the holes for the cuttings (do not force it in) and then firm them in gently. When using

Clearcut, take care to ensure that the cuttings are not damaged by the foil lid.
- *Keep the cuttings in a suitable place.*
Softwood cuttings.
Softwood cuttings need to be kept in a position with warmth (ideally 55°F-70°F), ventilation and humidity, but away from direct sunlight or cold draughts. Direct sunlight, even for two to three hours per day, can scorch these cuttings and prevent them from rooting. Therefore a south-facing position is usually too sunny, unless the cuttings can be shaded. An east- or west-facing position can be suitable, again so long as direct sunlight is avoided. A north-facing aspect is often ideal so long as the temperature and good light are maintained. Extra care in this aspect of taking cuttings will be rewarded with higher success rates. Compost should be kept moist (not wet) and water in containers should be

Always take cuttings from healthy, actively growing parent plants.

kept topped up. In Clearcut maintenance, such as watering, is not necessary.

Hardwood cuttings.

Although these cuttings are taken in autumn and winter, they are best protected from frost. Therefore keep pots or other containers under glass, i.e. in a cold greenhouse or cold frame, or at least protected from wind, perhaps under a fence or wall (preferably south- or west-facing), or plunged into insulating materials such as peat or vermiculite.

Take care with some poisonous plants.

It is wise to remember that several varieties of common house and garden plants are poisonous. Generally this is not a problem, but when taking cuttings there can be an opportunity for sap or small pieces of plants to come into contact with skin or household items. Therefore, do be cautious. Always wash your hands and rinse tools and work surfaces after handling these plants. The following list includes some of the plants to be careful with:

Azalea
Codiaeum (Croton)
Datura
Dieffenbachia
Euphorbia
Fatshedera
Gloxinia
Hedera helix
Hoya
Nerium
Philodendron

Tips and ideas

The following are additional tips and ideas to help avoid common problems with cuttings and to help identify the faults when cuttings fail to root.

Signs that a cutting will root when in a rooting medium:
- the cutting stays healthy green and unwilted;
- no signs of pests and diseases;
- signs of thickening or 'callousing' on stems, particularly at the base or on leaf nodes.

For hardwood cuttings leaves will almost certainly fall off, so look for healthy stems and leaf buds. Stems under bark will retain a green colour and buds at leaf nodes will be green or pink and plump rather than shrivelled.

Signs that a cutting is unlikely to root:
- there is serious loss of colour or moisture content (withering);
- signs of rotting off of stem or leaves, or serious leaf drop;
- signs of pests or diseases such as grey mould on leaves or black mould on stems;

These semi-hardwood cuttings have shrivelled and are unlikely to root.

One of the first signs that a cutting will root is white callousing on stems or leaf nodes as on this dahlia cutting. Roots will form from these areas.

– no signs of thickening or 'callousing' after several weeks.

If cuttings continue to look healthy, particularly when in Clearcut, do not disturb them and be patient.

Plants that will not root from cuttings

One of the common causes of cuttings' failure to root is an attempt to use parts of plants which simply do not have the capability of forming roots from stems or leaves. Even though sometimes you can be lucky, the following are examples of things to avoid:

flowers from florists' arrangements;
ferns and palms (except via offsets);
plants growing from bulbs, corms or tubers such as Cyclamen.

Prunings versus cuttings

Not every piece removed from a plant makes a good cutting. Try to plan when and where to take cuttings rather than

being disappointed by poor results from bits and pieces knocked off by the cat or the vacuum cleaner. When you do have to prune or tidy your plants, keep cuttings in mind. Often cutting back a mature plant can at least produce new growth suitable for cuttings.

It is best to have cuttings of one plant variety together in one container.

Keep cuttings of one plant variety together in the same container

It is best to have cuttings of only one plant variety together in one container. This is because different plants root at different speeds and you should not disturb the slower plants in order to pot up the quicker rooting ones.

When taking bud, leaf or root cuttings in particular, keep track of which part of the plant is the top as the cutting will not root if inserted upside down into the rooting medium. A good method for this is to make the bottom cut slanted and the top cut flat.

1. Stem cutting;
2. Leaf stem cutting;
3. Leaf bud cutting.

Many succulents root from leaves and leaf stems.

How to identify the correct type of cutting

As a general rule, the dominant structural parts of the plant give cuttings that will root.

Hence the appearance of the plant will give clues about the best type of cutting to take from it. If it is made up of a structure of stems with several leaves growing along each stem it is usually the stem which will root. If the plant is mostly formed from leaves, either with one leaf per short stem or several leaves all growing from the same point on short stems, then a leaf stem or leaf cutting may be correct.

Leaves that root are usually small, firm and fleshy. Plants with very thin or very large leaves usually root from stems. Stems that will root are usually at least of pencil thickness, fleshy and not hollow, and have nodes or joints where leaves joined the stem.

If you are unsure about the right type of cutting from a plant and cannot find out from the glossary on pages 36-56, a stem cutting is the best one to try as it is the most common.

Sometimes both stems and leaves from the same plant will root - particulary some houseplants and succulents - so try some of each to find the best method for you and your plants.

Potting up and cultivation

As soon as your cuttings are well rooted, they should be potted up into a good compost such as Levington, containing the right level of nutrients for an actively growing new plant. For both indoor and outdoor plants, always pot up cuttings and let them develop a good root system in a small pot before potting-up into a larger permanent pot or planting out into the garden. Never put a rooted cutting straight into a very large pot or into soil.

When to pot up

The amount of roots needed before potting up will vary according to the variety of the plant used and the size of the cutting. As a general rule: the larger the cutting, the more roots there should be before you can transfer it to its first pot. Disturbing a cutting too early or potting up too late can kill or seriously check the growth of the new plant.

For softwood cuttings, there should be several roots (three or four) at least one inch long. Ideally each root will also have smaller side shoots or root hairs which indicate a well developed new root system ready for transplanting.

For semi-hardwood and hardwood cuttings there should also be several roots, each at least two inches long and including side shoots.

Try to avoid damaging roots when transplanting in order to avoid disease and to allow the cutting to grow away quickly.

How to tell when cuttings are ready to pot up

This is a difficult but important part of taking cuttings and it is obviously dependent on the rooting medium used. First, be patient! Make sure that you have allowed enough time for rooting, at least three to four weeks or more depending on the plant and the time of year. For all cuttings look for firm, healthy stems and leaves. For cuttings in compost new growth of stems, leaves or side shoots can be an indication that rooting has taken place and they are ready for potting up. In water or Clearcut the roots will be visible.

However, if you are using pots or trays of compost, there are several ways to tell if rooting has occured:

- There is new growth such as new leaves or shoots.
- There are roots growing out of the drainage holes.

– If in single pots, carefully tap out the compost and look for roots.

You can also try gently tugging the cutting by its base: if it comes out of the compost easily, it is not rooted. (Check then for other relevant signs such as callousing, pests or disease). If it resists the tugging it probably has roots.

If you are rooting several cuttings together, try gently separating and removing one cutting to check progress, if you must.

For hardwood cuttings in trenches or frames outdoors, it is best to leave these undisturbed until at least late spring. New buds or other growth will indicate which ones have rooted, and these can be carefully lifted and potted up.

If you are using compost for rooting cuttings always make sure it is moist or, even better, watered thoroughly before removing cuttings, as this will help to reduce the risk of damage.

If roots are growing out of the bottom of the pot the cuttings are ready to be potted up separately.

If you are using Clearcut, make sure that the foil lid is peeled away before removing cuttings. Leave the gel around the roots when potting up, especially if it has begun to dry up, as it will give a benefit in transplanting.

Caring for your new plant

Once your rooted cutting has been removed from the rooting medium, pot it into a small pot (usually 3″) in a good potting or multi-purpose compost. It is important now to maintain sufficient quantities of moisture and plant food as the cutting becomes established. Always water the cutting after potting, but there after avoid overwatering or watering too frequently, as this is the most common cause of death or sickness in pot plants. A good compost should have enough nutrients to feed the plant for several weeks. However, after this you will need to feed the plant using one of several different methods in liquid or solid form such as Fisons Deep Feed, Fisons Long Lasting Feed, Jobes Spikes or Murphy Feed and Grow Mat.

Finally, continue to check for and treat any pests and diseases in order to keep your plants healthy and growing strongly. Soon they will be ready for you to take more cuttings.

Pests and diseases

It is important to keep cuttings free from pests and diseases while they are rooting.

Only a few pests or diseases attack cuttings in particular, but those that do can seriously affect rooting and cause death if they are not controlled. While prevention is always best, some problems can be treated.

The chart below has details on identification and treatment of most of the pests and diseases of cuttings.

1. Fungal diseases			
Disease	**Description of problem**	**Plants affected**	**Prevention and control**
Botrytis (grey mould)	Grey mould developing in spots and spreading to entire plant	Any	Use healthy plants. Treat cuttings with fungicide* before inserting. Improve warmth and ventilation. Remove all affected plant material
Powdery mildew	White powdery deposit mainly on leaves but also on stems and flowers	Any	Use healthy plants. Treat cuttings with fungicide* before inserting. Improve warmth and ventilation. Remove all affected plant material
Botrytis (black leg)	Blackening of whole or parts of cuttings, mainly the stem, leading to collapse and death	Many plants, particularly Pelargonium and Begonia	Use healthy plants. Treat cuttings with fungicide* before inserting. Improve warmth and ventilation. Remove all affected plant material
Rust	Brown powdery spots on underside of leaves	Many plants, particularly Pelargonium	Use healthy plants. Treat cuttings with fungicide* before inserting. Destroy all affected cuttings

* Recommended fungicides: Murphy Tumbleblite or Fisons Mildew & Blackspot Killer. Use pesticides as directed on packaging.

2. Pests

Pest	Description of problem	Plants affected	Prevention and control
Aphid *(greenfly, blackfly)*	Green or black flying or sucking insects on stems or leaves, often with a sticky deposit	Any	Remove pests and/or treat with insecticide.* Repeat as necessary
Leaf miner	Tiny grubs forming whitish-brown tunnels in leaves	Mainly Chrysanthemum	Use unaffected plants. Treat with insecticide* at first sign of attack and repeat as necessary
Mealy bug	Small fluffy white clusters on stems or underside of leaves	Many plants	Wipe off adults and treat plant with insecticide* to kill immature pests
Red spider mite	Tiny red sucking insect on stems or underside of leaves, often with a fine white webbing. Leaves become mottled and drop off	Any	Remove pests and/or treat with insecticide.* Repeat as necessary. Improve humidity around plant with daily misting
Scale	Small brown shells attached to stems or underside of leaves.	Many plants	Wipe off adults and treat plant with insecticide* to kill immature pests
Thrips	Tiny black or tan jumping insects on stems or leaves causing poor growth and distortion	Many plants, particularly Begonia and Fuchsia	Treat with insecticide* and repeat as necessary
Whitefly	White flying or sucking insects on stems or leaves, often with a sticky deposit	Any	Remove pests and/or treat with insecticide.* Repeated applications will be necessary

* Recommended insecticide* – Murphy Tumblebug, Fisons Insect Spray for Houseplants. Use pesticides as directed on packaging.

Cuttings guide

The plant pictures and lists in this section
are designed as a guide to the range of
plants suitable for softwood cuttings. While
the individual plants have been selected
with Clearcut in mind, all of the
information also applies to cuttings in any
rooting medium. In addition a success
rating has been given to indicate which
cuttings are easier or more difficult to root:
a = easy; b = moderate; c = difficult.

The guide is divided into five sections:
1. Houseplants, cacti and succulents
2. Garden plants
3. Shrubs
4. Climbers
5. Herbs
6. Alpines

There is also a section of other types of
plants to propagate in Clearcut.

Each section begins with photographs to
help identify representative plants and to
give information on how and when to take
cuttings in each case. There is also a full list
of plants in each section that are suitable for
rooting in Clearcut. These sections are
meant as a guide and are by no means
complete. If the general rules of cuttings
are followed, there are many other plants
to try in Clearcut. The 'weeks to root'
section indicates when you should see roots
starting to grow under ideal conditions
rather than when the cutting is ready to pot
up.

Because Clearcut is not recommended for
hardwood cuttings, these are not included
in this section. However, a selection of
shrubs suitable for softwood cuttings have
been listed. Remember that even with care
not all cuttings will root. Always take more
cuttings than you need and do not be put
off trying again if some fail to root.

Refer to the foregoing chapters for details
on how to take the recommended types of
cuttings.

Aphelandra
Zebra plant

Type of cutting: *stem*
No. of cuttings in pot: *3*
Weeks to root: *3-4*
Success rating in
Clearcut: *moderate*

Begonia
(caned stem type)

Type of cutting: *stem*
No. of cuttings in pot: *3*
Weeks to root: *2-3*
Success rating in
Clearcut: *easy*

Beloperone
Shrimp plant

Type of cutting: *stem*
No. of cuttings in pot: *3*
Weeks to root: *3-4*
Success rating in
Clearcut: *moderate*

Codiaeum
Croton (narrow leaf
varieties)

Type of cutting: *stem*
No. of cuttings in pot: *4*
Weeks to root: *3-5*
Success rating in
Clearcut: *easy*

Coleus
Flame nettle

Type of cutting: *stem*
No. of cuttings in pot: *3*
Weeks to root: *1-2*
Success rating in
Clearcut: *easy*

Columnea
Goldfish plant

Type of cutting: *stem*
No. of cuttings in pot: *4*
Weeks to root: *2-3*
Success rating in
Clearcut: *easy*

Crassula
(example: Jade plant)

Type of cutting: *stem*
No. of cuttings in pot: *3*
Weeks to root: *3-6*
Success rating in
Clearcut: *easy*

Dracaena marginata
Dragon plant

Type of cutting: *stem (tip)*
No. of cuttings in pot: *2*
Weeks to root: *3-4*
Success rating in
Clearcut: *easy*

Echeveria

Type of cutting: *entire leaf*
No. of cuttings in pot: *4*
Weeks to root: *2-3*
Success rating in
Clearcut: *easy*

Ficus elastica
Rubber plant

Type of cutting: *stem or bud*
No. of cuttings in pot: *1*
Weeks to root: *3-4*
Success rating in
Clearcut: *easy*

Gynura
Purple passion vine or velvet plant

Type of cutting: *stem*
No. of cuttings in pot: *3*
Weeks to root: *2-3*
Success rating in
Clearcut: *easy*

Opuntia
Prickly pear

Type of cutting: *sections or pads*
No. of cuttings in pot: *2*
Weeks to root: *3-4*
Success rating in
Clearcut: *easy*

Pelargonium grandiflora
Regal pelargonium

Type of cutting: *stem*
No. of cuttings in pot: *3*
Weeks to root: *3-4*
Success rating in
Clearcut: *moderate*

Peperomia

Type of cutting: *leafstem,
leaf*
No. of cuttings in pot: *4*
Weeks to root: *3-4*
Success rating in
Clearcut: *easy*

Philodendron scandens
Sweetheart vine

Type of cutting: *stem or
leafbud*
No. of cuttings in pot: *3*
Weeks to root: *3-4*
Success rating in
Clearcut: *easy*

Saintpaulia
African violet

Type of cutting: *leafstem*
No. of cuttings in pot: *4*
Weeks to root: *4-8*
Success rating in
Clearcut: *moderate*

Sansevieria
Mother-in-law's tongue

Type of cutting: *leaf-
section*
No. of cuttings in pot: *1*
Weeks to root: *5-6*
Success rating in
Clearcut: *easy*

Saxifraga
Mother of Thousands

Type of cutting: *offsets*
No. of cuttings in pot: *4*
Weeks to root: *1-2*
Success rating in
Clearcut: *easy*

Schefflera
Umbrella tree

Type of cutting: *stem*
No. of cuttings in pot: *3*
Weeks to root: *3-4*
Success rating in
Clearcut: *easy*

Schlumbergera
Christmas cactus

Type of cutting: *leaf*
No. of cuttings in pot: *4*
Weeks to root: *3-4*
Success rating in
Clearcut: *easy*

Senecio rowleyanus
Bead plant

Type of cutting: *stem
section*
No. of cuttings in pot: *6*
Weeks to root: *3-4*
Success rating in
Clearcut: *moderate*

Sinningia speciosa
Gloxinia

Type of cutting: *whole
leaf*
No. of cuttings in pot: *2*
Weeks to root: *4-5*
Success rating in
Clearcut: *moderate*

Tolmiea
Piggy-back plant

Type of cutting: *offset*
No. of cuttings in pot: *3*
Weeks to root: *3-4*
Success rating in
Clearcut: *easy*

Tradescantia
Inch plant, Wandering
Jew

Type of cutting: *stem*
No. of cuttings in pot: *4*
Weeks to root: *1-2*
Success rating in
Clearcut: *easy*

latin name (unless specified listing applies to all species)	common name	type of cutting	recommended no. of cuttings in pot	weeks to root	success rating in Clearcut
acalypha	copper leaf or monkey tail	stem	2	3-4	a
allamanda	golden trumpet	stem	2	3-4	b
aphelandra	zebra plant	stem	3	3-4	b
asplenium bulbiferum	spleenwort fern	plantlet	3	3-4	a
begonia	cane-stemmed	stem	3	2-3	a
	bushy	stem	3	3-4	a
	rex	leafstem	2	3-4	b
beloperone	shrimp plant	stem	3	3-4	b
callistemon	bottle brush tree	stem	2	3-4	a
chamaecereus	peanut cactus	stem	3	2-3	a
chlorophytum	spider plant or airplane plant	offsets	3	1-2	a
chrysanthemum	chrysanthemum or pot mum	stem (side shoots)	4	2-3	a
chrysanthemum frutescens	marguerite	stem	4	2-3	a
cissus antarctica	kangaroo vine	stem	4	3-4	a
cissus rhombifolia*	grape ivy	leaf bud	5	3-4	a
clerodendrum	bleeding heart vine	stem	3	2-3	a
codiaeum	croton (narrow leaf varieties)	stem	4	3-5	a
codiaeum	croton (broad leaf varieties)	stem	2	3-5	b
coleus	jacob's coat or flame nettle	stem	3	1-2	a
columnea	goldfish plant	stem	4	2-3	a
cordyline terminalis	red edge or dracaena	stem	2	3-5	a
crassula	crassula (incl. jade plant)	stem	3	3-6	a
crossandra	firecracker	stem	3	2-3	a
datura	angel's trumpet	stem (new shoots)	1	3-4	b
dianthus	carnation or pink	stem (non-flowering shoots)	5	3-4	a
dieffenbachia	leopard lily or dumb cane	stem tip	3	3-4	b
dipladenia	pink allamanda or mandevillea	stem or leaf bud	3	2-3	b
dracaena marginata (see also cordyline)	dragon or ribbon plant	stem (tip)	2	3-4	a
echeveria	echeveria	entire leaf	4	2-3	a
epipremnum aureum	devil's ivy, scindapsis or pathos	leaf stem	3	3-4	a

* avoid using the shoot tips of this plant as they are very soft and not suitable for cuttings.

latin name (unless specified listing applies to all species)	common name	type of cutting	recommended no. of cuttings in pot	weeks to root	success rating in Clearcut
euonymus	spindle	stem	4	3-5	a
euphorbia hermentiana	cathedral cactus	stem	2	3-4	a
euphorbia pulcherrima	poinsettia	stem	2	4-5	b
fatshedera lizei	ivy tree	stem	2	3-4	a
ficus benjamina	weeping fig	stem	3	3-4	b
ficus elastica	rubber plant	stem	1	3-4	a
ficus pumila	creeping fig	stem	3	3-4	a
ficus radicans	trailing fig	stem	3	3-4	a
fuchsia	fuchsia	stem	4	3-4	a
geranium (see pelargonium)					
gynura	purple passion vine or velvet plant	stem	3	2-3	a
hebe	hebe or veronica	stem	4	2-3	b
hedera helix	ivy	stem or leaf bud	5	3-4	a
hibiscus rosea sinensis	hibiscus	stem (new shoots)	3	3-4	b
hoya	wax plant	stem/bud	2	3-4	a
hydrangea	hydrangea	stem (new shoots)	3	3-4	b
hypoestes	polka dot plant	stem	4	3-4	b
impatiens	busy lizzie	stem	3	1-2	a
iresine	blood leaf or chicken gizzard	stem	3	2-3	a
jasmine	jasmine	leaf bud	4	4-5	b
kalanchoe	kalanchoe or flaming katy	stem or leaf stem or leaf	4	3-4	a
kleinia	candleplant	stem	3	3-4	a
lobivia	desert cacti	offsets	2	3-4	b
maranta leuconeura	prayer plant or rabbit's foot	leaf stem to include a leaf node	2	1-2	a
monstera deliciosa	swiss cheese plant	leafstem	1	4-6	b
nephrolepsis exaltata	boston fern	offsets	2	3-5	b
nerium	oleander	stem	3	3-4	b
opuntia	prickly pear	sections or pads	2	3-4	a
pelargonium grandiflora	regal pelargonium	stem	3	3-4	b
pelargonium peltatum	ivy leaf geranium	stem	4	3-4	a
pelargonium zonal	geranium	stem	4	2-3	b
pellionia	pellionia or satin vine	stem	3	2-3	a

latin name (unless specified listing applies to all species)	common name	type of cutting	recommended no. of cuttings in pot	weeks to root	success rating in Clearcut
peperomia	peperomia	leaf stem	4	3-4	a
peperomia caperata	peperomia	leaf	4	3-4	a
philodendron erubescens	red emerald	stem or leaf stem	3	3-4	a
philodendron scandens	sweetheart vine	stem or leaf bud	3	3-4	a
pilea cadierei	aluminium plant	stem	4	3-4	a
pilea microphylla	artillery plant	stem	4	3-4	a
plectranthus	swedish ivy or candle plant	stem or leaf bud	3	2-3	a
poinsettia (see euphorbia)					
rebutia	desert cacti	offsets	4	2-3	a
rhipsalidopsis	easter cactus	leaf	4	3-4	a
rhoicissus (see cissus)					
rochea	matchstick plant	stem	3	3-4	a
rosa mini	pot rose	stem tip	4	3-4	c
ruellia	ruellia	stem	3	2-3	a
saintpaulia	african violet	leaf stem	4	4-8	b
sansevieria*	mother-in-law's tongue	leaf section	1	5-6	a
saxifraga	mother of thousands	offsets	4	1-2	a
schefflera arboricola	umbrella tree	stem (tip or side shoots)	3	3-4	a
schlumbergera	christmas cactus	leaf	4	3-4	a
scindapsus pictus (see also epipremnum)	silver vine	stem	3	2-3	a
senecio rowleyanus	bead plant	stem section	6	3-4	b
setcreasia	purple heart	stem	3	3-4	a
sinningia speciosa	gloxinia	whole leaf	2	4-5	b
streptocarpus	cape primrose	leaf section	2	4-5	c
syngonium	white butterfly	stem	2	3-4	b
tolmiea	piggyback plant	offsets	3	3-4	a
tradescantia	inch plant	stem	4	1-2	a
zygocactus (see schlumbergera)					

* only green varieties will grow true to type from cutting

How to take a cutting from a Streptocarpus?
1. *Select a healthy adult leaf.*

2. *Cut sections of one inch or more in height across the leaf, including a main vein.*

3. *Dust base of the cutting with a rooting hormone.*

4. *Insert the cutting upright about halfway into the compost.*

Aster
Michaelmas daisy

Type of cutting: *stem*
Appropriate time of the
year: *May-June*
No. of cuttings in pot: *5*
Weeks to root: *3-4*
Success rating in
Clearcut: *moderate*

Ceratostigma

Type of cutting: *stem*
Appropriate time of the
year: *June-July*
No. of cuttings in pot: *5*
Weeks to root: *3-4*
Success rating in
Clearcut: *moderate*

Chrysanthemum

Type of cutting: *stem
(basal)*
Appropriate time of the
year: *January-May*
No. of cuttings in pot: *4*
Weeks to root: *3-4*
Success rating in
Clearcut: *easy*

Dahlia

Type of cutting: *stem*
Appropriate time of the
year: *February-May*
No. of cuttings in pot: *3*
Weeks to root: *2-3*
Success rating in
Clearcut: *easy*

Delphinium
Larkspur

Type of cutting: *stem*
Appropriate time of the
year: *May-June*
No. of cuttings in pot: *3*
Weeks to root: *2-3*
Success rating in
Clearcut: *moderate*

Dianthus
Carnation or Pink

Type of cutting: *stem*
Appropriate time of the
year: *March-October*
No. of cuttings in pot: *6*
Weeks to root: *2-3*
Success rating in
Clearcut: *easy*

Dimophorteca
Cape marigold

Type of cutting: *stem*
Appropriate time of the
year: *March-October*
No. of cuttings in pot: *4*
Weeks to root: *3-4*
Success rating in
Clearcut: *easy*

Fuchsia

Type of cutting: *stem*
Appropriate time of the
year: *March-May*
No. of cuttings in pot: *5*
Weeks to root: *3-4*
Success rating in
Clearcut: *easy*

Gypsophila
Baby's breath

Type of cutting: *stem*
Appropriate time of the
year: *April-September*
No. of cuttings in pot: *4*
Weeks to root: *3-4*
Success rating in
Clearcut: *moderate*

Lamium
Dead nettle

Type of cutting: *stem*
Appropriate time of the
year: *March-October*
No. of cuttings in pot: *4*
Weeks to root: *2*
Success rating in
Clearcut: *easy*

Lobelia
(perennial)

Type of cutting: *stem*
Appropriate time of the
year: *March-October*
No. of cuttings in pot: *4*
Weeks to root: *2-3*
Success rating in
Clearcut: *easy*

Vinca minor
Periwinkle

Type of cutting: *stem*
Appropriate time of the
year: *March-September*
No. of cuttings in pot: *5*
Weeks to root: *3-4*
Success rating in
Clearcut: *moderate*

latin name (·unless specified listing applies to all species)	common name	type of cutting	appropriate time of the year	recommended no. of cuttings in pot	weeks to root	success rating in Clearcut
anaphalis	anaphalis	stem	may/jun	5	4-5	b
anthemis	chamomile	stem	may/aug	5	3-4	b
antirhinum	snapdragon	stem	apr/may	5	2-3	b
artemisia lactiflora	white mugwort	stem	jun/jul	3	1-2	b
artemisia stelleriana 'nana'	dusty miller	stem	jul/aug	5	1-2	a
aster	michaelmas daisy	stem	may/jun	5	3-4	b
ballota	ballota	stem (lateral shoots)	jun/aug	4	3-4	a
brunnera macrophylla	brunnera	side shoots	may, sep	4	3-4	b
ceratostigma	ceratostigma	stem	jun/jul	5	3-4	b
chrysanthemum	chrysanthemum	stem (basal)	jan/may	4	3-4	a
dahlia	dahlia	stem	feb/may	4	2-3	a
delphinium	larkspur	stem	may/jun	3	2-3	b
dianthus	carnation or pink	stem	mar/oct	6	2-3	a
diascia	diascia	stem	mar/oct	4	3-4	a
dimorphotheca	cape marigold	stem	mar/oct	4	3-4	a
erigeron 'dimity'	fleabane	stem	may/jun	3	3-4	b
felicia	blue marguerite	stem	jun/aug	3	3-4	b
fuchsia	fuchsia	stem	mar/may	5	3-4	a
gazania	gazania	stem (basal)	jun/sep	3	3-4	b
gypsophila	baby's breath	stem	apr/sep	4	3-4	b
helichrysum	snow in summer	stem	jun/aug	4	3-4	a
lamium	dead nettle	stem	mar/oct	4	2	a
lobelia	lobelia (perennial)	stem	mar/oct	4	2-3	a
lupinus	lupin	stem (basal)	mar/may	3	2-3	b
lysimachia	loosestrife	stem	apr/sep	4	3-4	a
malva	mallow (perennial)	stem	mar/apr	3	3-4	b
mimulus	musk or monkey flower	stem	apr/may	4	3-4	b
nepeta	catmint	stem	apr/jul	4	3-4	a
oenothera	evening primrose	stem	may/jun	3	3-4	a
pelargonium	geranium	stem	mar/oct	4	4	a
penstemon	penstemon	stem	jul/sep	3	3-4	b
phlox paniculata	phlox	stem	mar/may	4	3-4	b
rudbeckia	coneflower	stem (basal in spring)	may/aug	4	3-4	b
scabiosa	scabious	stem	mar/may	3	3-4	b
scrophularia	figwort	stem	jun/jul	4	3-4	b
sedum	stonecrop	stem	apr/sep	4	3-4	a
stachys lanata	lamb's ear	stem	apr/jun	4	5-6	b

latin name (unless specified listing applies to all species)	common name	type of cutting	appropriate time of the year	recommended no. of cuttings in pot	weeks to root	success rating in Clearcut
verbena	vervain	stem	apr/jun	3	3-4	b
veronica	speedwell	stem	may/jun	4	3-4	b
vinca	periwinkle	stem	mar/sep	5	3-4	b
viola	pansy	stem (basal)	jun/aug	4	3-4	a

How to take a cutting from a Dianthus?
1. Choose a healthy young shoot, two to four inches long. Trim leaves from the lower half of the stem. Cut the stem to just below a leaf joint.

2. Dust the base of the cutting with a rooting hormone. Insert at least half of the cutting into the compost.

3. Enclose the pot with cuttings in a clear polythene bag to keep the compost moist and to protect the cuttings from moisture loss.

Cotoneaster

Type of cutting: *stem*
Appropriate time of the
year: *June-August*
No. of cuttings in pot: *4*
Weeks to root: *3-4*
Success rating in
Clearcut: *easy*

**Cryptomeria Japonica
'Elegans'**
Japanese cedar

Type of cutting: *stem*
Appropriate time of the
year: *June-September*
No. of cuttings in pot: *2*
Weeks to root: *5-6*
Success rating in
Clearcut: *easy*

Euonymus
Spindle tree

Type of cutting: *stem*
Appropriate time of the
year: *June-September*
No. of cuttings in pot: *4*
Weeks to root: *3-4*
Success rating in
Clearcut: *moderate*

Hebe
Hebe, Veronica

Type of cutting: *stem*
Appropriate time of the
year: *June-August*
No. of cuttings in pot: *4*
Weeks to root: *3-4*
Success rating in
Clearcut: *moderate*

Santolina
Cotton lavender

Type of cutting: *stem*
Appropriate time of the
year: *July-September*
No. of cuttings in pot: *4*
Weeks to root: *2-3*
Success rating in
Clearcut: *easy*

Weigela

Type of cutting: *stem*
Appropriate time of the
year: *July-August*
No. of cuttings in pot: *3*
Weeks to root: *3-4*
Success rating in
Clearcut: *easy*

latin name (unless specified listing applies to all species)	common name	type of cutting	appropriate time of the year	recommended no. of cuttings in pot	weeks to root	success rating in Clearcut
azalea japonica	azalea	stem	jun/jul	3	3-4	c
choysia	mexican orange	stem	jul/sep	3	4-5	b
cistus	rock rose	stem	jul/sep	4	4-5	b
cotoneaster	cotoneaster	stem	jun/aug	4	3-4	a
cryptomeria japonica elegans	japanese cedar	stem	jun/sep	2	5-6	a
cytisus	broom	stem	jun/jul	4	3-4	c
daphne	daphne	stem	jun/jul	4	3-4	c
deutzia	deutzia	stem	jun/jul	4	4-5	c
escallonia	escallonia	stem	jul/sep	4	3-4	b
euonymus	spindle tree	stem	jun/sep	4	3-4	b
forsythia	forsythia	stem	jul/sep	4	3	b
fuchsia	fuchsia (hardy species)	stem	may/sep	4	2-3	a
genista lydia	broom	stem	jun/aug	4	5-6	c
hebe	hebe, veronica	stem	jun/aug	4	3-4	b
hibiscus	tree hollyhock	stem	jun/aug	3	3-4	b
hydrangea	hydrangea	stem	jun/sep	3	3-4	a
lavatera	tree mallow	stem	may/jul	3	3-4	a
lavendula lanata	lavender	stem	jul/sep	5	3-4	c
lonicera	shrub honeysuckle	stem	jul/oct	5	4-6	b
magnolia soulangeana	magnolia	stem	jul/aug	2	4-5	c
potentilla fruticosa	cinquefoil, potentilla	stem	jul/sep	4	4-5	c
pyracantha	firethorn	stem	jul/aug	4	3-4	c
sambucus	elder	stem	aug/sep	3	2-3	b
santolina	cotton lavender	stem	jul/sep	4	2-3	a
senecio	senecio	stem	jul/aug	4	3-4	b
viburnum	viburnum	stem	jun/aug	2-3	3-4	c
weigela	weigela	stem	jul/aug	3	3-4	a

Clematis
Virgin's bower

Type of cutting: *stem*
Appropriate time of the
year: *July-August*
No. of cuttings in pot: *3*
Weeks to root: *3-4*
Success rating in
Clearcut: *difficult*

Hedera
Ivy

Type of cutting: *leaf bud*
Appropriate time of the
year: *May-September*
No. of cuttings in pot: *4*
Weeks to root: *2-3*
Success rating in
Clearcut: *easy*

Hydrangea petiolaris
Climbing hydrangea

Type of cutting: *stem*
Appropriate time of the
year: *August*
No. of cuttings in pot: *3*
Weeks to root: *4-6*
Success rating in
Clearcut: *moderate*

Lonicera
Honeysuckle

Type of cutting: *stem*
Appropriate time of the
year: *June-July*
No. of cuttings in pot: *3*
Weeks to root: *2-3*
Success rating in
Clearcut: *moderate*

Parthenocissus
Virginia creeper

Type of cutting: *stem*
Appropriate time of the
year: *July-August*
No. of cuttings in pot: *3*
Weeks to root: *3-4*
Success rating in
Clearcut: *moderate*

Passiflora
Passion flower

Type of cutting: *stem*
Appropriate time of the
year: *May-September*
No. of cuttings in pot: *3*
Weeks to root: *3-4*
Success rating in
Clearcut: *easy*

latin name (unless specified listing applies to all species)	common name	type of cutting	appropriate time of the year	recommended no. of cuttings in pot	weeks to root	success rating in Clearcut
actinidia kolomikta	actinidia	stem	jul/sep	3	3-4	c
clematis	virgin's bower	stem	jul/aug	3	3-4	c
hedera	ivy	leaf bud	may/sep	4	2-3	a
hydrangea petiolaris	climbing hydrangea	stem	aug	3	4-6	b
jasminum nudiflorum	winter jasmine	stem	mar/sep	4	3-4	c
jasminum officinale	climbing jasmine	stem (nodal)	jul/aug	4	3-4	b
lonicera	honeysuckle	stem	jun/aug	3	2-3	b
parthenocissus	virginia creeper	stem	jul/sep	3	3-4	b
passiflora	passion flower	stem	may/sep	3	3-4	a
stephanotis	stephanotis	stem/ leaf stem	jul/aug	3	4-5	c
vitis coignetiae	vine	stem/ leaf bud	mar/oct	2	3-4	b
wisteria	wisteria	stem	jul/aug	2	3-4	c

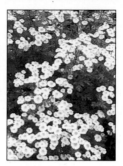

Artemisia dracunculus
Tarragon

Type of cutting: *stem*
Appropriate time of the
year: *July-August*
No. of cuttings in pot: *5*
Weeks to root: *3-4*
Success rating in
Clearcut: *easy*

**Chrysanthemum
parthenium**
Fever few

Type of cutting: *stem*
Appropriate time of the
year: *May-July*
No. of cuttings in pot: *4*
Weeks to root: *3-4*
Success rating in
Clearcut: *easy*

Mentha
Mint

Type of cutting: *stem*
Appropriate time of the
year: *May-September*
No. of cuttings in pot: *4*
Weeks to root: *1-2*
Success rating in
Clearcut: *easy*

Rosmarinus
Rosemary

Type of cutting: *stem*
Appropriate time of the
year: *July-September*
No. of cuttings in pot: *4*
Weeks to root: *4-5*
Success rating in
Clearcut: *moderate*

Salvia officinalis
Sage

Type of cutting: *stem*
Appropriate time of the
year: *May-July*
No. of cuttings in pot: *3*
Weeks to root: *4-5*
Success rating in
Clearcut: *moderate*

Thymus vulgaris
Thyme

Type of cutting: *stem*
Appropriate time of the
year: *June-July*
No. of cuttings in pot: *6*
Weeks to root: *5-6*
Success rating in
Clearcut: *difficult*

latin name (unless specified listing applies to all species)	common name	type of cutting	appropriate time of the year	recommended no. of cuttings in pot	weeks to root	success rating in Clearcut
artemisia dracunculus	tarragon	stem	jul/aug	5	3-4	a
chrysanthemum parthenium	fever few	stem	may/jul	4	3-4	a
laurus nobilis	sweet bay	stem	aug/oct	3	4-5	c
melissa officinalis	lemon balm	stem	may/jun	4	2-3	b
mentha	mint	stem	may/sep	4	1-2	a
myrtus communis	myrtle	stem	jul/aug	3	3-4	c
origanum vulgare aureum	golden marjoram	stem	jun/jul	4	2-3	b
rosmarinus	rosemary	stem	jul/sep	4	4-5	b
ruta graveolens	rue	stem	aug/sep	4	4-5	b
salvia officinalis	sage	stem	may/jul	3	4-5	b
thymus vulgaris	thyme	stem	jun/jul	6	5-6	c

How to take a cutting from Thymus?
1. *Choose a healthy young shoot.*
2. *Trim leaves from the lower half of the stem.*
3. *Use a well drained compost and firm lightly.*
4. *Use a dibber to make the holes for the cuttings in the compost. Insert at least half of the cutting into the compost.*
5. *Keep the compost moist, not wet.*

Achillea
Yarrow

Type of cutting: *stem*
Appropriate time of the
year: *June-September*
No. of cuttings in pot: *6*
Weeks to root: *2-3*
Success rating in
Clearcut: *easy*

Ajuga
Bugle

Type of cutting: *stem*
Appropriate time of the
year: *May-September*
No. of cuttings in pot: *4*
Weeks to root: *3-4*
Success rating in
Clearcut: *easy*

Hebe
Hebe, Veronica

Type of cutting: *stem*
Appropriate time of the
year: *June-September*
No. of cuttings in pot: *5*
Weeks to root: *3-4*
Success rating in
Clearcut: *easy*

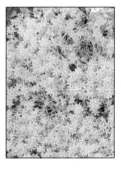

Lamium
Dead nettle

Type of cutting: *stem*
Appropriate time of the
year: *June-August*
No. of cuttings in pot: *5*
Weeks to root: *2-3*
Success rating in
Clearcut: *easy*

Saponaria
Soapwort

Type of cutting: *stem*
Appropriate time of the
year: *June-September*
No. of cuttings in pot: *5*
Weeks to root: *4-5*
Success rating in
Clearcut: *moderate*

Sedum
Stonecrop

Type of cutting: *stem*
Appropriate time of the
year: *June-July*
No. of cuttings in pot: *5*
Weeks to root: *2-3*
Success rating in
Clearcut: *easy*

latin name (unless specified listing applies to all species)	common name	type of cutting	appropriate time of the year	recommended no. of cuttings in pot	weeks to root	success rating in Clearcut
acaena	new zealand burr	stem	jul/aug	6	4-5	b
achillea	yarrow	stem	jun/sep	6	2-3	a
ajuga	bugle	stem	may/sep	4	3-4	a
cerastium tomentosum	snow-in-summer	stem	jun/jul	6	3-4	a
chiastophyllum oppositifolium	chiastophyllum	stem	jul/aug	4	3-4	b
chrysanthemum nipponicum	chrysanthemum	stem	may/jun	5	3-4	a
dianthus	carnation or pink	stem	jun/jul	6	2-3	a
diascia	diascia	stem	may/jun	6	3-4	a
eriophyllum	eriophyllum	stem	jun/jul	5	3-4	b
gypsophila	baby's breath	stem	may/jun	6	3-4	b
hebe	hebe or veronica	stem	jun/sep	5	3-4	a
helianthemum	rock rose	stem	aug/sep	6	3-4	c
lamium	dead nettle	stem	jun/aug	5	2-3	a
lychnis	maltese cross	stem	jun/jul	5	3-4	b
phlox	phlox	stem	may/jun	6	3-4	b
saponaria	soapwort	stem	jun/sep	5	4-5	b
sedum	stonecrop	stem	jun/jul	5	2-3	a
silene	campion or catchfly	stem	may/jun	5	3-4	b

latin name (unless specified listing applies to all species)	common name	type of cutting	appropriate time of the year	recommended no. of cuttings in pot	weeks to root	success rating in Clearcut
allium porrum	leek	pips or 'grass'	aug/nov	12	2-3	b
citrus	orange	pips	mar/oct	3	4	b
cynara scolymus	globe artichoke	suckers	apr/nov	3	3-4	a
fragaria	strawberry	runner	aug/sep	2	1-2	a
lilium	lily	bulblets or scales	jul/oct	7	2-3	a
lycopersicon	tomato	stem	mar/sep	3	1-2	a
persea americana	avocado	seed	mar/sep	1	6-8	b